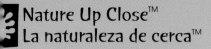

Nature Up Close™
La naturaleza de cerca™

Owls Up Close
Los búhos

Katie Franks
Traducción al español:
Ma. Pilar Sanz

PowerKiDS press™ & **Editorial Buenas Letras**™
New York

Published in 2008 by The Rosen Publishing Group, Inc.
29 East 21st Street, New York, NY 10010

First Edition

Editor: Jennifer Way
Book Design: Kate Laczynski
Photo Researcher: Nicole Pristash

Photo Credits: Cover, pp. 1, 5, 7, 9 (inset) 11, 13, 15, 17, 19, 21, 24 © Studio Stalio; p. 9 (main) © Shutterstock.com; p. 23 by Alessandro Bartolozzi.

Cataloging Data

Franks, Katie.
    Owls up close–Los búhos / Katie Franks; traducción al español: Ma. Pilar Sanz. — 1st ed.
        p. cm. — (Nature up close–La naturaleza de cerca).
    Includes index.
    ISBN 978-1-4042-7678-9 (library binding)
    1. Owls—Juvenile literature. 2. Spanish language materials I. Title.

Manufactured in the United States of America

Websites: Due to the changing nature of Internet links, PowerKids Press and Buenas Letras have developed an online list of Web sites related to the subject of this book. This site is updated regularly. Pleas use this link to access the list: www.powerkidslinks.com/nuc/owl/

Contents

The Owl 4

Night Hunters 8

Owl Families 20

Words to Know 24

Index 24

Contenido

Los búhos 4

Cazadores nocturnos 8

Familias de búhos 20

Palabras que debes saber........24

Índice 24

Owls are birds. Owls are known for flying during the night.

Los búhos son aves. Los búhos son conocidos por volar durante la noche.

5

Here is the inside of an owl's body. Some of its parts are the **skull**, the heart, the **lungs**, the wings, and the **claws**.

Este es el cuerpo de un búho por dentro. Algunas partes del cuerpo de los búhos son el **cráneo**, el corazón, los **pulmones**, las alas y las **garras**.

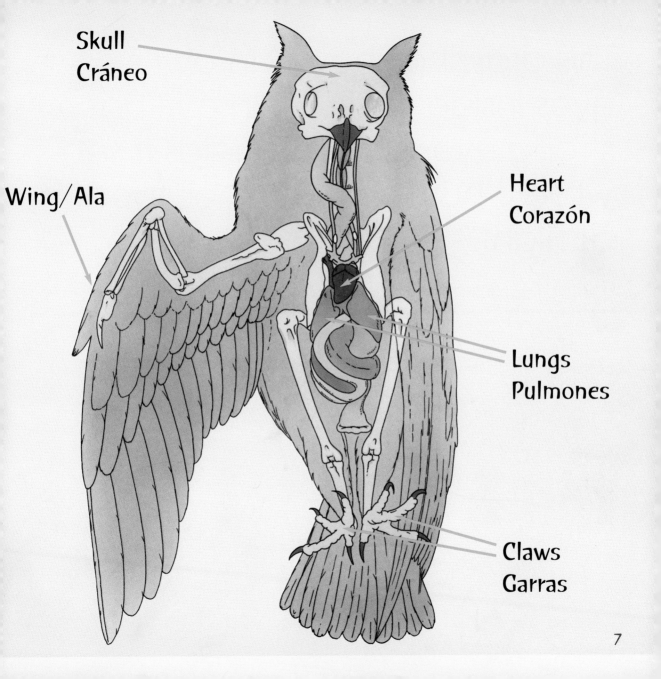

Skull
Cráneo

Wing/Ala

Heart
Corazón

Lungs
Pulmones

Claws
Garras

7

This drawing shows an owl's eyes inside its skull. An owl has strong eyesight that helps it see while it hunts, or catches food, at night.

Esta ilustración muestra el interior del cráneo de un búho. Los búhos tienen muy buena vista. Esto los ayuda a atrapar su comida durante la noche.

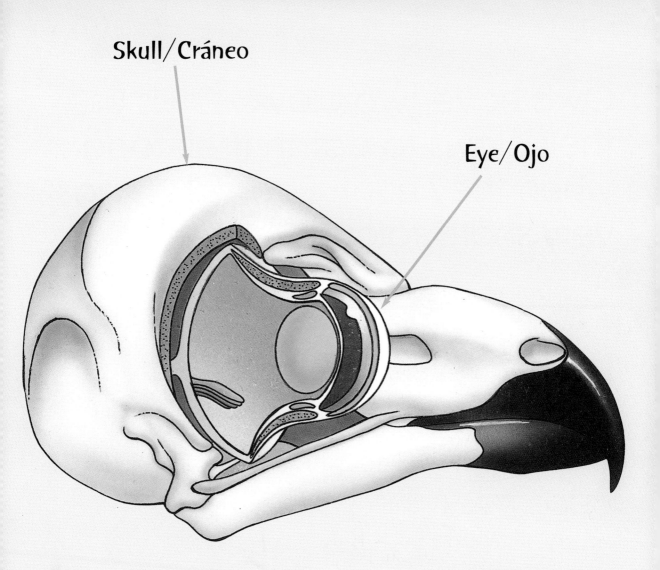

Skull/Cráneo

Eye/Ojo

Owls have two claws. Owls use their claws to catch their food when they hunt. Each claw has very sharp talons.

Los búhos tienen dos garras. Las garras los ayudan a atrapar su comida. Las garras tienen uñas muy filosas.

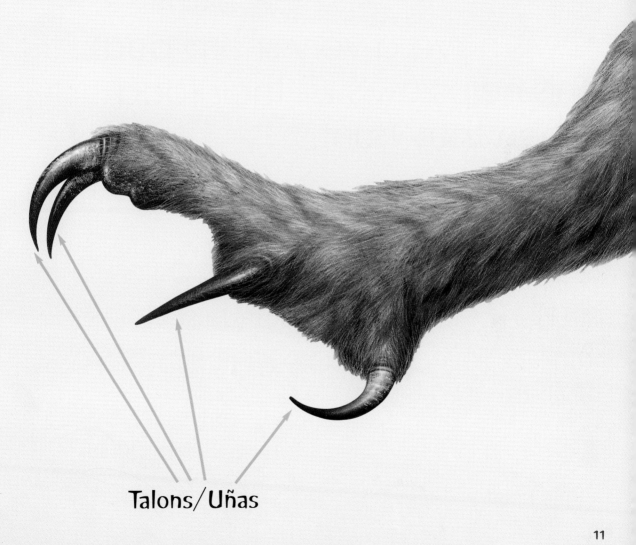

Talons/Uñas

Owls have a very sharp **beak**. This helps owls kill their food when they hunt.

Los búhos tienen un **pico** muy filoso. Esto los ayuda a matar los animales que cazan para comer.

Owls hunt many different kinds of small animals. This owl is catching a mouse.

Los búhos cazan muchos tipos de pequeños animales. Este búho está atrapando un ratón.

There are even owls that hunt fish. This owl caught a fish right out of the water!

¡Algunos búhos incluso atrapan peces! ¡Este búho pescó un pez en el agua!

17

After an owl catches some food, it brings the food back to the nest to feed its family.

Después de cazar, los búhos llevan la comida al nido. Ahí, alimentan a su familia.

The female, or girl, owl lays eggs. These eggs soon hatch, or break open, and baby owls come out.

Las búhos hembra ponen huevos. Después de unos días, estos huevos se rompen y nacen los búhos bebé.

Owls live all over the world. There are many different kinds of owls. Here are a few of them.

Las búhos viven en todo el mundo. Hay muchos tipos de búhos. Aquí puedes ver algunos de ellos.

Snowy Owl/Búho de las nieves

Great Horned Owl/Búho virginiano

Great Gray Owl/Cárabo lapón

Barn Owl/Búho de campanario

Words to Know / Palabras que debes sabe

beak / (el) pico

claw/(la) garra

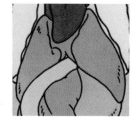

lungs/(los) pulmones

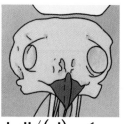

skull/(el) cráneo

Index

C
claws, 6, 10

F
food, 8, 10, 12, 18

N
night, 4, 8

S
skull, 6, 8

Índice

C
comida, 8, 10, 12, 18
cráneo, 6, 8

G
garras, 6, 10

N
noche, 4, 8